STOP OVERTHINKING

MINDFULNESS CAN BE YOURS

Choose To Live Mindfully
Every Single Day

Lyle Paul

Table of Contents

Chapter 1: How Will You Choose To Live Your Life? 6

Chapter 2: How To Play The Long Game In Life 8

Chapter 3: 6 Ways To Master Your Emotions 10

Chapter 4: Why Having Lesser Things Actually Makes You Happier .. 15

Chapter 5: How To Focus on Creating Positive Actions 19

Chapter 6: How To Use Affirmations For Success 22

Chapter 7: Practicing Gratitude for Increased Happiness and Satisfaction 24

Chapter 8: Things That Spark Joy 26

Chapter 9: Stop Being a Slave To Old Beliefs 29

Chapter 10: Do The Painful Things First 32

Chapter 11: Making Sky The Limit 34

Chapter 12: 20 Positive Affirmations For Men 36

Chapter 13: To Make Big Gains, Avoid Tiny Losses 40

Chapter 14: 3 Ways To Calm The Emotional Storm Within You 43

Chapter 15: 6 Ways To Get Full Attention From People Around You 47

Chapter 16: Get Rid of Worry and Focus On The Work 52

Chapter 17: 8 Habits That Can Kill You 56

Chapter 18: Being Mentally Strong 61

Chapter 19: *Happy People Give Freely* 63

Chapter 20: Saying Yes To Things 65

Chapter 21: 7 Ways To Discover Your Strengths 70

Chapter 22: Happy People are Okay with Not Being Okay 75

Chapter 23: Live Life To The Fullest 77

Chapter 24: What To Do When You Feel Like Your Work is not Good Enough 79

Chapter 25: Meditate to Rewire Your Brain for Happiness 82

Chapter 26: Overcoming Your Fears 84

Chapter 27: How To Deal With Impatience..................................... 87
Chapter 28: What Are You Measuring In Your Life? 90
Chapter 29: Develop Mental Toughness In The Face of Adversity 93
Chapter 30: *How to Face Difficulties in Life* 96
Chapter 31: How Not To Control Everything................................ 98
Chapter 32: 10 Habits Of Happy Kids 101
Chapter 33: Five Habits That Can Make Someone Like You........... 105
Chapter 34: 10 Habits Of Happy People 109
Chapter 35: 3 Steps To Choose Mind Over Mood......................... 113
Chapter 36: Stop Thinking and Start Doing 117

Chapter 1:
How Will You Choose To Live Your Life?

How will you choose to live your life? This is something that only you have the power to decide.

We all want different things. As individuals, we are all unique and we have our own ideas about what it means to live a meaningful life. Some treasure family, friends, and relationships above all else, while others prioritise money, material things, careers, and productivity. There is no right or wrong to pursue or place any of these things on a pedestal. If your dream is to build a multi-billion dollar company, then go ahead and chase that dream. If you prioritise just being as stress-free as possible, to do as little work as you can, well you can choose to structure your life in such a way as well. As long as it works for you and that you are happy doing so, I would say go for it.

Sure, your priorities might change as you get older and wiser. Embrace that change. We are not always met to move in a linear fashion in life. We should learn to live like water, being fluid, ever-changing, ever-growing, ever-evolving. Our interests, priorities, passions, all change as we move from one stage of life to the next.

Some only realise that they might want to focus on relationships at a certain point in their lives, some might only want to start a family when they reach a certain age. The point is that we never truly know when is the time when we might feel ready to do something, as much as well tell ourselves that we will know.

The best thing we can do for ourselves right now, in this very moment, is to do what we think is best for us right now, and then to make tweaks and adjustments along the way as we travel down that road faithfully.

Trying to plan and control every aspects of our lives rarely ever works out how we imagined it. You see, life will give us lemons, but it can also give us durians. We might get thrown off the road through unexpected changes. Things that challenge our beliefs and our priorities. Health issues, family tragedies, financial meltdowns, natural disasters, these are things that we can never plan for. We may either choose to come out of these things with a clearer plan for our next phase of life, or we may choose to give up and not try anymore.

All of us have the power to choose how we want to live our lives in this very moment. The worst thing you can do right now is not know what your priorities are and to just cruise through life without having at least a short-term vision on what you want to get out of it.

Take the time to reflect every single day to work on that goal, however scary or simple it may be. Never take your eye off the post and just keep traveling down that path until you reach a fork in the road.

Chapter 2:
How To Play The Long Game In Life.

Playing the long game in life is forming or shaping your life so that you control certain aspects of it. You should constantly strive for self-improvement and try to push yourself a little more each day. You are starting your day early and making sure that this day fulfills most of our tasks. Build strategies for career growth and development. Also, make sPlaying the long game in life is taking control of your future in a way that everything is planned. You have to be mindful of everything. Identifying what makes you happy, energized, and focused is a chance to prepare everything for the long term. To form the long game in your life means taking small steps of success in life for yourself. You need to strategize every move of yours.

It would be best if you were above average in gaining knowledge to predict the outcome of your move. If you want to plan long-term success in life, you need to understand the situations according to your needs. Always keep your mind open for excessive knowledge. Be hungry for it. Take steps towards self-improvement. Socialize with people who are more knowledgeable or experienced than you are. Learning should always be one of the priorities. Challenge yourself for more daily. As it's said, "if you are the smartest person in the room, you are in the wrong room." Understand that you will always need more to expand in life and be successful in life.

It would be best to keep in mind that not every step of yours will go as planned. Get yourself ready for rejection. You should not be scared of getting a rejection, but take it as a constructive opportunity to build yourself stronger for the next time. Your part should be fulfilled correctly. Hard work should be done, and the right choices should be made. In this case, advice should be taken too. You should not completely rely on someone, but a companion can be comforting. Always appreciate your co-workers and superior. That will help you in the future and your long-term game for success in life. Just keep in mind that the fear of rejection is useless.

Shaping your path is a difficult task and a very important opportunity. When you are forming your way of life, one of the most important things will be the type of people you will meet. You should be careful about the kind of people that surround you. As it is said, "one bad company can ruin all." This is true in a sense. Keep supportive and smart people by your side. Your long-term friendship or relationship can affect your life in many ways. It may change the outcome completely. Now, we would not want just anyone to come and take that part. That is why choosing the best people to surround you matters the most.
ure to have lots of fun in between the work. In the end, your hard work will pay off, and everything will feel like it was worth doing all the work for.

Chapter 3:
6 Ways To Master Your Emotions

As reported by Psychology Today, psychology's answer to the question of "What is emotional mastery?" Has evolved over the last century. Early American psychology embraced the "James-Lange Theory," which held that emotions are strictly the product of physiology (a neurological response to some external stimuli). This view evolved when the "Cannon-Bard Theory" asserted that the brain's thalamus mediates between external stimuli and subjective emotional experience.

The concept of emotional mastery wasn't introduced until the 1960s with the Schachter-Singer experiment, where researchers gave participants a dose of a placebo "vitamin." Participants then watched colleagues complete a set of questionnaires. When the colleagues responded angrily to the questionnaires, the participants felt angry in turn. But when the colleagues responded happily, the participants also felt happy. The study's results implied a connection between peer influence and the felt experience of emotion.

The idea that emotions are influenced by outer as well as inner stimuli was furthered by psychiatrist Allen Beck, who demonstrated that thoughts, peer influence and circumstance shape emotions. Beck's research formed the foundation of modern-day cognitive-behavioral therapy, the gold standard of emotional mastery as it's understood today.

The Role Of Emotional Mastery In Life And Society

Feelings and emotional mastery play a role in our subjective experience and interpersonal relationships.

- **Emotions unify us across cultural lines.** There are six basic emotions that are universal in all cultures: happiness, sadness, fear, anger, surprise and disgust. We all experience these feelings, although there are cultural differences regarding what's an appropriate display of emotion.

- **Emotions govern our sense of well-being.** Since emotions are a product of our experiences and how we perceive those experiences, we can cultivate positive emotions by focusing on them. There are 10 "power emotions" that cultivate emotional mastery by creating a base of positive affect. When we incorporate even small doses of gratitude, passion, love, hunger, curiosity, confidence, flexibility, cheerfulness, vitality and a sense of contribution, we set the stage for feeling good about ourselves.

- **Emotional mastery supports healthy relationships.** When you're able to demonstrate emotions that are appropriate to the situation, you're able to nurture your relationships. When you don't know how to master your emotions, the opposite occurs: You might fly off the handle at minor annoyances or react with anger when sadness is a more appropriate response. Your emotional response affects those around you, which shapes your relationships for better or worse.

Learning how to master your emotions is a skill anyone can build in six straightforward steps.

1. Identify what you're really feeling

The first step in learning how to master your emotions is identifying what your feelings are. To take that step toward emotional mastery, ask yourself:

- What am i really feeling right now?
- Am i really feeling…?
- Is it something else?

2. Acknowledge and appreciate your emotions, knowing they support you

Emotional mastery does not mean shutting down or denying your feelings. Instead, learning how to master your emotions means appreciating them as part of yourself.

- You never want to make your emotions wrong.
- The idea that anything you feel is "wrong" is a great way to destroy honest communication with yourself as well as with others.

3. Get curious about the message this emotion is offering you

Emotional mastery means approaching your feelings with a sense of curiosity. Your feelings will teach you a lot about yourself if you let them. Getting curious helps you:

- Interrupt your current emotional pattern.
- Solve the challenge.
- Prevent the same problem from occurring in the future.

4. Get confident

The quickest and most powerful route to emotional mastery over any feeling is to remember a time when you felt a similar emotion and handled it successfully. Since you managed the emotion in the past, surely you can handle it today.

5. Get certain you can handle this not only today, but in the future as well

To master your emotions, build confidence by rehearsing handling situations where this emotion might come up in the future. See, hear and feel yourself handling the situation. This is the equivalent of lifting emotional weights, so you'll build the "muscle" you need to handle your feelings successfully.

5. Get excited and take action

Now that you've learned how to master your emotions, it's time to get excited about the fact that you can:

- Easily handle this emotion.
- Take some action right away.
- Prove that you've handled it.

Learning emotional mastery is one of the most powerful steps you can take to create a life that's authentic and fulfilling.

Chapter 4:
Why Having Lesser Things Actually Makes You Happier

How many of you feel like spending money to acquire more stuff would make you happier because you believe having more things would bring you happiness and life satisfaction?

Now I'm not talking about basic necessities such as food, toiletries, or household appliances that you would actually use on a daily basis for the betterment of your own lives.

I'm talking about a constant need to purchase things as you go shopping at a mall, such as clothes, jackets, ornaments, cups, gadgets, bags, shoes, watches. Or even random stuff that you won't really use or need as you go on various shopping platforms online, especially during huge sale days like black friday or some other major holiday where discounts are abundant and you believe that if you don't buy this now that you are missing out on a great deal.

You might not notice this at the start, but before you know it, your house is starting to feel cluttered as every inch of your house is filled stuff with no place to put them. You might even start going to IKEA to buy shelves and cupboards to house these items in places where you will probably never see or touch them again in the foreseeable future. And they end up hidden there collecting dust.

Not to mention that all these incessant buying has also costed you money over the years.

What was once a clean home with a nice living space has turned into a cramped box of unwanted items that don't bring benefit or betterment to your lives.

How many of you can relate to that? Because that is what I used to do.

Just a few years back, when i wanted to buy clothes i would literally ransack the whole discount section of a particular store and checkout 10s of clothes in one shopping trip. And before i knew it my wardrobe was filled with so many clothes that i had a hard time going through them or deciding what i wanted to wear. And I also realised that i didn't really like most of what i had bought. Which lead to more buying. The same went for my obsession for gadgets. After a year i had so many iPads and iPhones that i did not know what to do with them that costed my thousands of dollars.

When I woke up one day and looked around my house, i realised that i regretted most of the purchases I made and that all these stuff was actually making me very unhappy.

So I did what made sense to me at the time, I started decluttering.

I went through each and every item in my house from my wardrobe to my bedroom, to my study and living room. And with each item held in my hand i asked myself 3 questions: "do i really need this?" "does this make me happy?" and "can someone else make better use of this item?"

And as i started sorting i realised that 70% of my things were stuff that i do not need and will not use. and only 30% of them actually brought me some sort of joy. The most prominent being the clothes i always wore even when i had countless others to choose from.

As I began donating to salvation army and discarding the junk, my house became less and less messy and cramped. And what remained was not only more space, but things that I had an emotional attachment to. Things that brought me a sense of joy when i loooked at them or touched them. The extra space also brought me a sense of peace that there were no hidden junk in cupboards and the space I had could put to better use rather than housing useless things.

This decluttering process was not only therapeutic but necessary for me. For the first time i felt that having lesser things actually made me happier. And That i didnt have to spend my way to achieve happiness. I also realised that what I had already in my house was more than I would ever need and that this is my sacred space that i should only fill with things that are meaningful to me.

What changed for me is that these days when i go shopping, I don't have the urge to spend money on things just because anymore. I end up gravitating towards shops that sells plants, fishes because those are what brings me joy these days. Living things that I have to care for with love and dedication.

This change in wanting lesser things has not only made me happier but also saved me money in the process.

I just want to end off by saying that having more things will never make you happy, but making more friends and being grateful for what you already have can give u the happiness you have been searching for.

Chapter 5:
How To Focus on Creating Positive Actions

Only a positive person can lead a healthy life. Imagine waking up every day feeling like you are ready to face the day's challenges and you are filled with hope about life. That is something an optimist doesn't have to imagine because they already feel it every day. Also, scientifically, it is proven that optimistic people have a lower chance of dying because of a stress-caused disease. Although positive thinking will not magically vanish all your problems, it will make them seem more manageable and somewhat not a big deal.

Positive thinking is what leads to positive actions, actions that affect you and the people around you. When you think positively, your actions show how positive you are. You can create positive thinking by focusing on the good in life, even if it may feel tiny thing to feel happy about because when you once learn to be satisfied with minor things, you would think that you no longer feel the same amount of stress as before and now you would feel freer. This positive attitude will always find the good in everything, and life would seem much easier than before.

Being grateful for the things you have contributed a lot to your positive behavior. Gratitude has proven to reduce stress and improve self-esteem. Think of the things you are grateful for; for example, if someone gives you good advice, then be thankful to them, for if someone has helped you with something, then be grateful to them, by being grateful about minor things, you feel more optimistic about life, you feel that good things have always been coming to you. Studies show that making down a list of things you are grateful for during hard days helps you survive through the tough times.

A person laughing always looks like a happy person. Studies have shown that laughter lowers stress, anxiety, and depression. Open yourself up to humor, permit yourself to laugh even if forced because even a forced laugh can improve your mood. Laughter lightens the mood and makes problems seem more manageable. Your laughter is contagious, and it may even enhance the perspective of the people around us.

People with depression or anxiety are always their jailers; being harsh on themselves will only cause pain, negativity, and insecurity. So try to be soft with yourself, give yourself a positive talk regularly; it has proven to affect a person's actions. A positive word to yourself can influence your ability to regulate your feelings and thoughts. The positivity you carry in your brain is expressed through your actions, and who doesn't loves an optimistic person. Instead of blaming yourself, you can think differently, like "I will do better next time" or "I can fix this." Being optimistic about the complicated situation can lead your brain to find a solution to that problem.

When you wake up, it is good to do something positive in the morning, which mentally freshens you up. You can start the day by reading a positive quote about life and understand the meaning of that quote, and you may feel an overwhelming feeling after letting the meaning set. Everybody loves a good song, so start by listening to a piece of music that gives you positive vibes, that gives you hope, and motivation for the day. You can also share your positivity by being nice to someone or doing something nice for someone; you will find that you feel thrilled and positive by making someone else happy.

Surely you can't just start thinking positively in a night, but you can learn to approach things and people with a positive outlook with some practice.

Chapter 6:
How To Use Affirmations For Success

Affirmations are best described as a self-help strategy that is used to promote self-confidence and belief in your abilities. There might come a million instances where you felt like you needed to affirm yourself, and there would be many moments when you have probably affirmed yourself without even realizing it. Simple sentences like "I've got what it takes" or "I believe in my ability to succeed" shift your focus away from the perceived inadequacies or failures and direct your focus towards your strengths. While affirmations may not be a magic bullet for instant success, they generally work as a tool for shifting your mindset and achieving your goals.

Neuroplasticity, or our brain's ability to adapt and change to different circumstances throughout our lives, makes us understand what makes affirmations work and how to make them more effective. Creating a mental image beforehand of doing something that you're scared of, like acing a nerve-wracking interview or bungee jumping to conquer your fear of heights, can encourage your brain to take these positive affirmations as fact, and soon your actions will tend to follow.

Repeating affirmations can help you boost your confidence and motivation, but you still must take some action yourself. Affirmations are a step towards the change, not the change itself. They can also help you to achieve your goals by strengthening your confidence by reminding you that you're in control of your success and what you can do right now to achieve it. Affirmations give you a list of long-standing patterns and beliefs, and it makes you act as if you've already succeeded. Understand that affirmations alone can't produce a change in every situation. You have to take some actions too along with them. Similarly, affirming your traits can also help you see yourself in a new light.

To get the most benefits from affirmations, start a regular practice and make it a habit. Say affirmations upon waking up and getting into bed; give them at least 3-5 minutes. Repeat each of your affirmations ten times, focus on the words that leave your mouth. Believe them to be true while saying them. Make it a consistent habit. You have to be patient and stick with your practice, and it might take some time before you see evident changes. Practicing affirmations can also activate the reward system in your brain, which can impact how you experience both emotional and physical pain. The moment you start managing your stress and other life difficulties, it would help you promote faith in yourself and boost self-empowerment.

Chapter 7:
Practicing Gratitude for Increased Happiness and Satisfaction

Much scientific evidence has shown that gratitude has far-reaching effects on our health. When people are thankful and are good with things as they are, their physical health reflects that. They're more likely to exercise, eat better, and take care of their health. Researchers over the years point to lower stress, reduced pain, and improved immune systems due to being thankful. Even better blood pressure and positive effects on the heart have been linked to gratitude.

Gratitude has a strong positive impact on psychological well-being as well. It increases self-esteem, enhances positive emotions, and makes us more optimistic. When we feel deep happiness, our bodies are producing all sorts of wonderful chemicals. Keller explains more specifically how rewarding it is for our bodies.

In 2018 and 2019, Finland ranked No. 1 in The United Nation's (UN) World Happiness Report. It's worth pausing to think about why Finland, Norway, Sweden, Denmark, and Iceland often rank at the top for the happiest people in the world. The UN report is a survey of global happiness that ranks 156 countries by respondent ratings of their own lives.

Therefore, Scandinavians themselves are determining their levels of happiness. It's pretty high. They appreciate a functioning society in which they have economic security and in which social institutions support everyone, not just a few. Yet, there is something else. The Swedes use the word "lagom" to describe a kind of moderation, a just enough-ness they value.

They don't chase happiness or work overtime for months at a time. By and large, they are accepting and content. They remain grateful for a healthy work-life balance, take breaks during the workday, and have a high standard of living. They also have low corruption and a high level of social trust. As a result of this satisfaction and contentment, they feel their lives have value. They have less pressure, less stress, and more time for what they enjoy.

Activate Gratitude Regularly

The best way to make gratitude a habit is not to wait for special moments. Some people have been told by their therapists they can keep stress and anxiety at bay by keeping a gratitude journal. Journaling every day is also correlated with an increase in happiness.

But if you're not ready for that kind of commitment, there's an easy way to begin on your road to being grateful. Just pay attention. Start identifying things you might take for granted. Then, take a moment to be thankful for them. Be sure to consider positive actions and events that might seem small, common-place, or inconsequential.

Chapter 8:
Things That Spark Joy

I'm sure you've heard the term "spark joy", and this is our topic of discussion today that I am going to borrow heavily from Marie Kondo.

Now why do I find the term spark joy so fascinating and why have i used it extensively in all areas of my life ever since coming across that term a few years ago?

When I first watched Marie Kondo's show on Netflix and also reading articles on how this simple concept that she has created has helped people declutter their homes by choosing the items that bring joy to them and discarding or giving away the ones that don't, I began my own process of decluttering my house of junk from clothes to props to ornaments, and even to furniture.

I realised that many things that looked good or are the most aesthetically pleasing, aren't always the most comfortable to use or wear. And when they are not my go to choice, they tend to sit on shelves collecting dust and taking up precious space in my house. And after going through my things one by one, this recurring theme kept propping up time and again. And i subconsciously associated comfort and ease of use with things that spark joy to me. If I could pick something up easily without hesitation to use or wear, they tend to me things that I gravitated to naturally, and these things began to spark joy when i used them. And when i started getting rid of things that I don't find particularly pleased to use, i felt my house was only filled with enjoyable things that I not only enjoyed looking at, but also using on a regular and frequent basis.

This association of comfort and ease of use became my life philosophy. It didn't apply to simply just decluttering my home, but also applied to the process of acquiring in the form of shopping. Every time i would pick something up and consider if it was worthy of a purpose, i would examine whether this thing would be something that I felt was comfortable and that i could see myself utilising, and if that answer was no, i would put them down and never consider them again because i knew deep down that it would not spark joy in me as I have associated joy with comfort.

This simple philosophy has helped saved me thousands of dollars in frivolous spending that was a trademark of my old self. I would buy things on the fly without much consideration and most often they would end up as white elephants in my closet or cupboard.

To me, things that spark joy can apply to work, friends, and relationships as well. Expanding on the act of decluttering put forth by Marie Kondo. If the things you do, and the people you hang out with don't spark you much joy, then why bother? You would be better off spending time doing things with people that you actually find fun and not waste everybody's time in the process. I believe you would also come out of it being a much happier person rather than forcing yourself to be around people and situations that bring you grief.

Now that is not to say that you shouldn't challenge yourself and put yourself out there. But rather it is to give you a chance to assess the things you do around you and to train yourself to do things that really spark joy in you that it becomes second nature. It is like being fine tuned to your 6th sense in a way because ultimately we all know what we truly like and dislike, however we choose to ignore these feelings and that costs us time effort and money.

So today's challenge is for you to take a look at your life, your home, your friendships, career, and your relationships. Ask yourself, does this thing spark joy? If it doesn't, maybe you should consider a decluttering of sorts from all these different areas in your life and to streamline it to a more minimalist one that you can be proud of owning each and every piece.

Chapter 9:
Stop Being a Slave To Old Beliefs

Life has a beginning for everyone. Everyone has a different life. Everyone has a different belief. Everyone has different brains and different observations. You are that everyone. You are different in every aspect possible except the fact that you are only human life to a billion others.

We humans, as a species have lived history through a certain set of rules. Modern and civilized cultures live with some social decorum and follow some societal beliefs and rituals. But who imposed these laws on us?

Who made these rituals so important for everyone, as if we cannot survive without them? There is no justification for most of these beliefs that are still being practiced to date.

Humans have also the same ways of adapting to thins like other animals. They tend to repeat things to perfect or learn them.

We have practiced so many pointless beliefs and conditions for so long that we are unwilling and unable to even try to think aside them.

We are so scared to look around these beliefs and shake things up a bit to create newer and better outcomes for us and others. But we still feel liable and a slave to this tendency to follow whatever is being imposed on us. No!

You are a free soul. You were born a free soul. You were given a unique mind and you should act like you still have one. You can think of bigger and better ways to make your life easier and more meaningful.

Look at a bird. They start taking lessons from other birds, but when they are finally in the air for the first time, they are now free to do anything they can ever wish to do.

You are also a free bird. You have everything you want to create new beliefs of your own where you don't have to justify or answer to anyone because now you have a person to fall back on. And that person is You!

What if you started a cult today, and someone came and asked you to justify it. Do you think you owe that person an answer? I don't think so!

Because you are a free individual who can anything he or she wants, only if it doesn't hurt anyone else around you.

You started your life alone and you will die alone. So why not live it alone too. I am not saying to give up on all relations. But you should make up your own beliefs if you are not OK with the previous ones.

Don't argue! You cannot force your opinion on anyone else, just like you are not obligated to follow anyone else's.

So from this day in your life. Make a vow to yourself, that you will take every day of your life as if it were a new life and you will discover newer things this time. This will help you find a newer purpose and will eventually create a new ambition for others to follow.

Chapter 10:
Do The Painful Things First

There are a lot of secret recipes to be happier; one of them is; seek what's painful first. Sure, this may sound a little ironic, but you will be surprised to know that all scientific research is behind this. Behavioral scientists discovered that one of the most effective ways to create an enjoyable experience is to stack the painful parts of the experience early in the process. For example, if you're a doctor, a lawyer, accountant, etc., it's better to break bad news first and then finish with the good news. This will give the clients a more satisfying experience since you start poorly then end on a solid note instead of starting well and ending badly.

There's a couple of crucial reasons why we should do the painful things first. We know that we have limited willpower during the day, and we also know that the most painful activities or tasks are sometimes the most difficult ones. So if we complete the things we find the most difficult first, we'll be exerting less energy on less complicated activities for the rest of the day. Scientific studies show that our prefrontal cortex (creative part of the brain) is the most active the moment we wake up. At the same time, the analytical parts of our brain (the editing and proofreading parts) become more active as the day goes on.

Another reason to do the painful activities firsthand after you wake up is that you would be freed from all the distractions and tend to do these tasks more quickly. If you delay the complex tasks, it will only come back to bite you. Starting with only one task for a day can be enough, as it could lead you to achieve more of them as time goes by. Things like building a new business, losing weight, or learning a new skill require pain and slow work in the beginning to get momentum. But after some persistence, you will likely see your improvements. Behavioral psychology suggests that we're more likely to lead a happier life if we're making improvements over time. Anthony Robbins once said, "If you're not growing, you're dying."

Making slow but gradual improvements is where persistency comes in. It's going to be painful and frustrating initially, and you won't learn a new language in an instant, or your business won't thrive immediately. But when you decide to sacrifice your short-term pleasure for a future pay-off, you will get to enjoy the long-term benefits over a sustained period. Stop avoiding what's hard; embrace it for your long-term happiness.

Chapter 11:
Making Sky The Limit.

Your attitude determines everything, whether it's in your personal life or your professional one. You ask any millionaire or billionaire how they got on top of their game and how they got to where they are, and they will undoubtedly tell you that they mastered their mind before mastering their game of success. So, the question arises, what exactly do we need to do to get to the next level? Some people strive for bigger things and achieve their goals against all odds, and they are not at all constrained by conventional thinking. Irrespective of their area of interest and chosen fields, they have certain experiences and characteristics in common. We now look at some of the things that we need to maintain to have a sky's-the-limit mindset.

Mastering your mind for the sky's-the-limit mindset comes up with the most crucial key, accepting rejection. We all have faced and experienced rejection at some point in our lives. But if we let it consume us and allow it to fester, it can lie dormant and negatively affect our lives. There are a million examples in front of us who faced rejections but are now extremely successful. Take J.K. Rowling; she was a single mother living on welfare and struggling to support her child. She faced repeated rejections but never gave up. Her first Harry Potter book got sold for about €4000. Now she's even richer than the Queen of England.

We all want to be successful, but are we ready to put in the blood, sweat, and tears it takes to get there? Thinking big and doing big takes willpower and a lot of work, the amount of work that isn't a piece of cake for everyone. Malcolm Gladwell tells us that if you want to be an expert or champion in something, you must be willing to devote 10,000 hours to it (90 minutes a day for 20 years). And if you're doing so, you need to feel passionate about it too. Van Gogh sold only one piece during his lifetime, but his passion drove him to paint almost 900 works.

Understand that we are flawed creatures, and we are bound to make mistakes. Bill Gates may be the world's richest man, but even he says that his failures served him as a great learning tool. Thomas Edison took between 1,000 to 10,000 tries before creating the world-changing invention. See your failures as a part of your journey. Without them, you won't be able to succeed much. And if they can fail, what makes you think you can't?

Be confident in your abilities and trust yourself. Surround yourself with good people who will help you accomplish things. People who would clap at your success and help you during your failures. Welcome every opportunity with open arms. Find the good in every situation, no matter how bad it looks on the outside. Every experience has its value, identify and cherish those experiences that serve you with opportunities to learn. The only thing stopping you from being successful is yourself.

Chapter 12:
20 Positive Affirmations For Men

A positive affirmation is a statement about yourself that is phrased in the positive, present tense. It reflects an area of your life, emotions, or belief system that you want to improve or change. The potential benefits of affirmations are vast. Positive affirmations empower you to become the best version of yourself. They inspire you to act in ways that help you fulfill your potential. You can use positive affirmations to reprogram negative thoughts into positive beliefs. The ability to reprogram your beliefs about yourself has the potential to transform your life completely.

For an affirmation to be effective, it needs to meet four criteria.

Each positive affirmation you use should be:

1. **Worded in the present tense**
2. **Positive**
3. **Specific**
4. **Personal**

You can create your own positive affirmations using this four-step framework. The benefits of affirmations are dramatically increased when you have created it yourself from an existing negative belief. Let's say you had a belief that you are unsuccessful in your job. Where focus goes, energy flows. If you keep feeding this belief, it will manifest as truth.

When you understand this, you can see how our thoughts really do shape our reality. Instead, you can use this belief as an opportunity to grow. Take that statement and switch it to its positive opposite. Rather than thinking: 'I am terrible at my job, I'll never get a promotion, my boss hates me,' you now think 'I am great at my job, I love what I do, and I always put 100% effort into every task

Whether you choose to formulate your own positive affirmations or use the ones I have created for you below, you must cultivate a daily practice. The best times to practice are first thing in the morning and last thing at night (or whenever you feel that you need to repeat them to start feeling better). During these times, your mind is more open and will absorb the statements on a deeper level.

It is best if you say them out loud while looking in the mirror. Speaking them to yourself affirms that you trust in yourself, and you believe the statements to be true. If speaking them out loud is not possible, you can say them in your mind. Writing them out a few times a week is also beneficial. Try getting a journal specifically for this purpose. Another technique that you might find useful is to pin the written affirmations to the mirror or refrigerator, where you will see them often.

When you are just beginning with this practice, it may be easy to forget, so set an alert on your phone or in your calendar to remind you. Here are 20 examples of positive affirmations relating to different areas of life.

Choose the ones that resonate most with you. Once you feel that you have integrated those particular statements, you can select or create new ones for other areas you want to improve.

Confidence and Self-Esteem

1: "I feel confident in every situation."

2: "I like who I am."

3: "I am a good person."

4: "I am great at helping people."

5: "I feel valued by my friends and family."

Inner Strength and Resilience

1: "I meet each new challenge with enthusiasm."

2: "I am strong and stable."

3: "I think I can, so I can."

4: "No matter what happens, I can handle it."

5: "I am powerful."

Positivity and Joy

1: **"I radiate joy to everyone I meet."**

2: **"I see the best in people."**

3: **"In the present moment there are no issues, only peace."**

4: **"Happiness is a choice; today, I choose to be happy."**

5: **"I have the power to turn negative thoughts into positive beliefs."**

Career and Success

1: **"I deserve success."**

2: **"I can succeed at whatever I choose."**

3: **"I am good at my job, and I love what I do."**

4: **"I have great ideas."**

5: **"I am innovative and tenacious."**

I hope that my guide to positive affirmations for men has provided you with a solid foundation for designing your perfect practice. Remember, to reap the benefits of affirmations, you should say them out loud every day and write them out a few times a week. Use any of my examples of positive affirmations, or for extra power, try creating your own using my framework. If you commit to a daily practice, you will soon notice the benefits in your career, relationships, emotional resilience, sense of self-worth, and confidence.

Chapter 13:
To Make Big Gains, Avoid Tiny Losses

Life is a process of adding and subtracting. We add the things that make us better and make life easier. We put aside the things that prove to be a pebble in the shoe.

There is a flaw in human effort and our concept for success. We think that we can achieve more if we focus harder on getting better. We think that if we are not getting worse, we are on the right track. But I can assure you, we are heavily mistaken.

The more we focus on bigger gains, the more we overlook the small things we stop caring about. We give up on relations, hobbies, ethics, love, and the million other losses that we don't measure on the same scale.

We can achieve the same amount of things, the same scale of success, and still, be the better person that we want to be. But we don't need to not work on the smaller details of this successful journey.

Let's say you have achieved it all and now you look back a decade or two. Do you think you won't regret the things that could have been saved in this whole process? But you chose not to or didn't care enough for them, and now you are rich in the pocket but poor in every other sense.

They say money can buy you anything, but it can never buy you happiness. You can have all the money in the world but you can't make sure if you won't ever have any regret.

We all are a creator. We make things, sometimes for ourselves and sometimes for people around us. Sometimes we make things better for us that then prove to be good for someone else as well. But also do things in a way that doesn't affect anyone else in a bad way. At least not deliberately.

Bad things happen, but most of the time we are the reason for them to happen in the first place. We are so devoted to the greater good that we neglect the small things we lose in the process.

Check it with yourself, if you are so devoted to being a better person than you were yesterday, and you have achieved more than yesterday. Then why do you still repeat the small mistakes and take the small losses?

You have to understand the concept of losses over gains. If you invest some money into something, and you are at a small loss every other day, then you can't justify the big profits you might gain some days later.

It is the constant concern to keep away from the small misfortunes or mistakes that might leave you into yet another breakdown. If you truly want to be a free and successful person, you need to have confidence in whatever you do will certainly give you more and more and it won't come at the cost of a single thing.

Take the mantra, reduce your losses and your gains will gain volumes in no time.

Chapter 14:
3 Ways To Calm The Emotional Storm Within You

When emotions are already intense, it's often hard to think about what you can do to help yourself, so the first thing you need to work on is getting re-regulated as quickly as possible. Here are some fast-acting skills that work by changing your body's chemistry; it will be most helpful if you first try these before you're in an emotional situation, so you know how to use them.

1. Do a forward bend

This is my favourite re-regulating skill. Bend over as though you're trying to touch your toes (it doesn't matter if you can actually touch your toes; you can also do this sitting down if you need to, by sticking your head between your knees). Take some slow, deep breaths, and hang out there for a little while (30 to 60 seconds if you can). Doing a forward bend actually activates our parasympathetic nervous system – our 'rest and digest' system – which helps us slow down and feel a little calmer. When you're ready to stand up again, just don't do it too quickly – you don't want to fall over.

2. Focus on your exhale with 'paced breathing'

It might sound like a cliché but breathing truly is one of the best ways to get your emotions to a more manageable level. In particular, focus on making your exhale longer than your inhale – this also activates our parasympathetic nervous system, again helping us feel a little calmer and getting those emotions back to a more manageable level. When you inhale, count in your head to see how long your inhale is; as you exhale, count at the same pace, ensuring your exhale is at least a little bit longer than your inhale. For example, if you get to 4 when you inhale, make sure you exhale to at least 5. For a double whammy, do this breathing while doing your forward bend.

These re-regulating skills will help you to think a little more clearly for a few minutes, but your emotions will start to intensify once more if nothing else has changed in your environment – so the next steps are needed too.

3. Increase awareness of your emotions

In order to manage emotions more effectively in the long run, you need to be more aware of your emotions and of all their components; and you need to learn to name your emotions accurately. This might sound strange – of course you know what you're feeling, right? But how do you know if what you've always called 'anger' is actually anger, and not anxiety? Most of us have never really given our emotions much thought, we just assume that what we think we feel is what we actually feel – just like we assume the colour we've always called 'blue' is actually blue; but how do we really know?

Sensitive people who have grown up in a pervasively invalidating environment often learn to ignore or not trust their emotional experiences, and try to avoid or escape those experiences, which contributes to difficulties naming emotions accurately. Indeed, anyone prone to emotion dysregulation can have trouble figuring out what they're feeling, and so walks around in an emotional 'fog'. When you're feeling 'upset', 'bad' or 'off', are you able to identify what emotion you're actually feeling? If you struggle with this, consider each of the following questions the next time you experience even a mild emotion:

- What was the prompting event or trigger for the feeling? What were you reacting to? (Don't judge whether your response was right or wrong, just be descriptive.)

- What were your thoughts about the situation? How did you interpret what was happening? Did you notice yourself judging, jumping to conclusions, or making assumptions?

- What did you notice in your body? For example, tension or tightness in certain areas? Changes in your breathing, your heart rate, your temperature?

- What was your body doing? Describe your body language, posture and facial expression.

- What urges were you noticing? Did you want to yell or throw things? Was the urge to not make eye contact, to avoid or escape a situation you were in?

- What were your actions? Did you act on any of the urges you noted above? Did you do something else instead?

Going through this exercise will help you increase your ability to name your emotions accurately. Once you've asked yourself the above questions, you could try asking yourself if your emotion fits into one of these four (almost rhyming) categories: mad, sad, glad, and afraid. These are terms I use with clients as a helpful starting point for distinguishing basic emotions, but gradually you can work on getting more specific; emotions lists can also be helpful.

Chapter 15:

6 Ways To Get Full Attention From People Around You

The long-term success of someone's life depends on getting the attention of others. Those others can include your teammates, your boss, your life partner, your clients, etc. But how? A person may ask. You cannot get promoted without getting your boss's attention, and your work cannot get appreciated by your teammates without awareness. To lead a healthy personal life, one may need to give attention to and from one's life partner, and of course, without the attention of your clients, how will your business survive?

Fortunately, there is plenty of research on how a human brain works and how it can focus on something. A lot of people have been researching about gaining people's attention for a long time now.

By some researchers, attention has been considered the "most important currency anybody can give you," although attention does make a person feel loved, it also gains your success. Fame can even come through negative attention, but it comes with hate as its price, whereas true and long-term success comes from positive attention. Here are six ways to get full attention from people around you.

1. Stand In A Central Position

When you are at a social gathering or a party, place yourself in a central position. Try to appear more friendly to new people, invite them over to your group, this way people will like you more. When you speak, they will pay attention—standing in a prominent place where everybody can see and talk to you easily will gain you more alert. Be being friendly to new individuals, and you will feel connected to others. Just be confident the whole time, and try to blend well with others and stand in a prominent place; this way, you will get more attention.

2. Leave Some Mystery!

Do you know what Zeigarnik Effect is? This effect suggests that the human brain tends to remember those things more, which is incomplete, as the question in their brain arises how? Where? And what?

This kind of technique is often used by professionals in business meetings, audience-oriented presentations. However, you can also use it in your daily life. When you introduce yourself to someone, don't just spill everything about yourself right away. Give the tiniest bit of pieces of information about something interesting, don't give the details just yet;

wait for someone to ask for the details. And someone will surely ask, and you will get the desired attention.

3. **Use Body Language**

Most of us know how to communicate verbally, but do you know how to communicate non-verbally? Because non-verbal communication is as important as verbal communication. Maintain positive body language, and if you sit back slouched and give some closed-off vibes, it is less likely that you would catch someone's attention. To see some attention, you need to bring more positivity in your conversation and your body language. Don't cross your arms and legs when talking to someone; face them with an open posture and stand with confidence. Don't avoid eye contact but don't overdo it; try to maintain eye contact with everyone around you for a while. This will show your confidence and also builds a connection with others. Be relaxed confidently. Smiling while talking to someone indicates your friendliness and makes them feel welcome; this way, they feel comfortable and give you their undivided attention, but everybody would avoid talking to you if you look moody.

4. **Leave An Impression**

It is the subconscious habit of a human being to think more about the people who left a good impression on them, try to engage their senses like touch, hear, or vision. Who doesn't like fashion nowadays? Try to wear something fashionable and decent, the kind of outfit that will likely leave a good impression on others. You can also wear something that has a different color or a twist to it. Speak confidently and in a clear voice. You can also put on a lovely perfume, cologne; try not to go overboard with this as nobody likes too much smell even if it is good.

5. **Having A Hype Team**

Having a hype team can easily capture a lot of attention; when you are in a not so formal setting, bring along your friends, surely they will be more than happy to excite you up. When you talk about your achievements among other people, it may seem to some that you are simply bragging. Still, when someone else talks about your accomplishments, it increases the interest of other people in you and gains you some positive attention.

6. **Find A Way To Sell Yourself Without Bragging**

A hype team is not always an option, but selling yourself without bragging is also something that needs to be done. What you don't need to discuss is;

- Your bank balance
- The expensive things you own
- Your occupation
- Your achievement

Conclusion

Brag through storytelling, and everybody loves an inspiring story. A successful person with a humble background always gains some attention. Attention plays an essential role in our lives, and you need to put a bit of effort into gaining it.

Chapter 16:

Get Rid of Worry and Focus On The Work

Worry is the active process of bringing one's fears into reality.
Worrying about problems halts productivity by taking your mind off the work in hand.
If you're not careful, a chronic state of worrying can lead you down a dark path that you might find hard to get out of.

Always focus on the required work and required action towards your dream.
Anything could happen, good or bad,
but if you remain focused and do the work despite the problems,
you will through with persistence and succeed.

Always keep your mind on the goal,
your eyes on the prize.
Have an unwavering faith in your abilities no matter what.

Plan for the obvious obstacles that could stand in your way,
but never worry about them until you have to face them.
Tackle it with confidence as they come and move forward with pride.

Problems are bound to arise.

Respond to them necessarily along the way, if they actually happen.

After all, most worries never make it into reality.

Instead focus on what could go right.

Focus on how you can create an environment that will improve your chances of success.

You have the power over your own life and direction.

As children we dreamed big.

We didn't think about all the things that could go wrong.

As children we only saw the possibilities.

We were persistent in getting what we wanted no matter the cost.

As adults we need to be reminded of that child-like faith.

To crush worry as if it were never there.

To only focus on the possibilities.

You cannot be positive and negative at the same time.

You cannot be worrying and hopeful of the future.

You cannot visualise your perfect life while worrying about everything that could go wrong.

Choose one.

Stick to it.

Choose to concentrate on the work.

The result will take care of your worries.

Catch yourself when you feel yourself beginning to worry about things.

Instead of dwelling on the problem, choose to double down on the action.
Stay focused and steadfast in the vision of your ultimate goal.

The work now that you must do is the stepping stones to your success.
The work now must have your immediate attention.
The work now requires you to cast worry aside in favour of concentration and focus.

How many stepping stones are you away?
What is next?
Push yourself every single day.
Because only you have the power to create your future.
If not, things will remain the same as they have always been.

Always have a clearly defined goal,
A strong measure of faith,
And an equally strong measure of persistence and grit.
These are the ingredients to creating the life you want.
A life of lasting happiness and success.

Take control instead of accepting things as they are.
Reject anything else that is not the goal that you've set for yourself.
Whatever goal you set, ten times it, and focus on it every day.
The focus will keep your mind on the work until you succeed.
There will be no time to worry when you are too busy taking constant action.

Always have the belief In your heart and soul that you will succeed.

Never let a grain of doubt cast a shadow in your eventual path to victory.

Focus is key to all.

What you focus on, you will create.

Worrying is worse than useless,

it is DETRIMENTAL to your future.

Take control of your thoughts.

When worry pops it's ugly head, force it out with a positive thought of your future.

Don't let the negative illusions of worry live rent-free in your mind.

You are in control here.

Of what you watch,

What you read,

What you listen too

And what you think.

What you think of consistently will become.

Focus on what you want, and how to get there is crucial for lasting happiness and success.

Chapter 17:
8 Habits That Can Kill You

Toxic habits in our lives which when left unchecked can lead us to an early grave. We may not be aware of it but it is most definitely eating away at us slowly; like a frog gradually boiling to his death. These invisible yet harmful habits will start appearing in your life if you don't start taking note of it.

Here are 8 habits that can kill you if you're not careful:

1. Being a workaholic.

Man shall eat from the sweat of his brows. Our income pays our bills and puts food on the table. This infers that work is good for it is the backbone on which our survival is pegged upon. It is however not a license to bite more than you can chew. Drowning yourself at work is dangerous for your health.

There is a breaking point for every person. Workaholism is a habit that depressed people do to drown their misery. With only so much that you can handle, you will lose touch with the world if you work without a break. Workaholics are not hard workers who work to make ends meet. They are obsessed with work so that they can forget their problems.

If you are a workaholic who uses business to distract you from your problems, you run the risk of sinking to depression. Take note if stress disorders or suicidal thoughts start to appear. It may be time to seek help to deal with your problems head on instead of masking them in busyness.

2. <u>Isolating yourself from others.</u>

Withdrawal is a red flag any day, anytime. The moment you begin finding comfort in solitude, not wanting to associate with anyone, a problem is in the offing. However, there are times when you will need time alone to meditate and seek peace within yourself.

It is during withdrawal that suicidal thoughts are entertained and sometimes executed. When one isolates themselves from the rest of the world, he becomes blind and deaf to the reality on the ground. You seemingly live in a separate world often mistaken as one of tranquility and peace.

To fight isolation, always find a reason to be around people you share common interests with. It could be sports, writing, acting, or watching. This will help keep off loneliness.

3. <u>Drug and substance abuse.</u>

Drug abuse is a pitfall that many youths have fallen into. It will lead you to an early grave if you do not stop early enough. Apart from the long-term side effects on the health of addicts, drug abuse rips addicts off morality. Most of them become truants, finding themselves on the wrong side of the law and society.

Among the many reasons drug addicts give for drug abuse is that drugs give solace from the harsh world, some kind of temporary blissful haven which the soul longs for. It is unjustifiable to enter into such a health-damaging dungeon to contract respiratory diseases, liver disease, kidney damage, and cardiovascular diseases.

Be careful if you seek drugs as a way to escape from your troubles. If you look closely, most of these people do not end up in a good place after abusing these substances. Seek a healthier alternative instead to let off steam instead.

4. <u>Judging yourself by the standards of others.</u>

As Albert Einstein rightly put it; if we judge a fish by its ability to climb a tree, it will live its whole life believing it is stupid. It is erroneous to use other people's measurement of success to judge your own. This is not to say that you should not be appreciating the achievements of others, but as you do so, give yourself time and space for growth.

The pressure that comes with conforming to your peers' standards can push you down a dark path. Society can be so unforgiving for the faint-hearted. Once you are inside the dark hole of hopelessness, the air of gloom hangs over your head and it can lead you to an early grave. Everyone will forsake you when you fail even after trying to be like them.

5. <u>Being in the wrong company.</u>

Bad company ruins good morals. This truth is as old as civilization. It is not rocket science on how powerful the power of influence from friends is. When in the wrong company, you will be tagged into all sorts of activities they do. Isn't that a direct ticket to hades?

When you lose the power to say No and defend your integrity, morals, and everything that you believe in, then all hell will break loose on you. You would have handed your hypocrite friends the license to ruin your life. Not only will the wrong company ruin your life but also assassinate your character. Keep safe by fleeing from the wrong company when you can before it is too late.

6. <u>Lying.</u>

It looks simple but what many people do not consider is the effect of character assassination caused by a simple lie. Lying makes you unreliable. One client or employer will tell another one and before you know it no one wants anything to do with you.

It may not physically kill you but it will have the power to close all possible open doors of opportunities. Why not be genuine in your dealings and win the trust of your employers and clients? You should jealously protect your reputation because any assault at it is a direct attack on your integrity.

7. <u>Lack of physical exercise.</u>

A healthy body is a healthy mind. To increase your longevity, you need to have a healthy lifestyle. It is not always about the posh vehicle you are driving or the classy estate you live in. How physically fit you are plays a big role in determining your productivity.

You need to walk out there in the sun, go for a morning run, lift weights, do yoga and kegel exercises, or go swimming. Your body needs to be maintained by exercise and not dieting alone. It seems ignoble to be a field person but its benefits are immense.

8. <u>Poor nutritional habits.</u>

The risks of poor nutrition are uncountable. Overeating and obesity come from these habits. Few people pay attention to what they eat, ignorant of the consequences that follow.

Malnutrition and obesity are opposites but stemming from one source – poor nutrition. The eminent danger can no longer be ignored.

According to statistics from the World Health Organization, worldwide obesity has nearly tripled since 1975. In 2016 alone, more than 1.9 billion adults were overweight. The world health body acknowledges that the developmental, economic, social, and medical impacts of the global burden of malnutrition are serious and lasting, for individuals and their families, communities, and countries.

This has come as a shocker to us but it would not have been so if people paid attention to their nutrition habits.

All these 8 habits that can kill you are avoidable if caution is taken. The ball is in your court. Consider carefully whether you want to make a conscious decision to take responsibility and eliminate these damaging habits. You have the power to change if you believe in yourself.

Chapter 18:
Being Mentally Strong

Have you ever wondered why your performance in practice versus an actual test is like night and day? Or how you are able to perform so well in a mock situation but just crumble when it comes game time?

It all boils down to our mental strength.

The greatest players in sports all have one thing in common, incredibly strong beliefs in themselves that they can win no matter how difficult the circumstance. Where rivals that have the same playing ability may challenge them, they will always prevail because they know their self-worth and they never once doubt that they will lose even when facing immense external or internal pressure.

Most of us are used to facing pressure from external sources. Whether it be from people around us, online haters, or whoever they may be, that can take a toll on our ability to perform. But the greatest threat is not from those areas... it is from within. The voices in our head telling us that we are not going to win this match, that we are not going to well in this performance, that we should just give up because we are already losing by that much.

It is only when we can crush these voices that we can truly outperform our wildest abilities. Mental strength is something that we can all acquire. We just have to find a way to block out all the negativity and replace them with voices that are encouraging. to believe in ourselves that we can and will overcome any situation that life throws at us.

The next time you notice that doubts start creeping in, you need to snap yourself out of it as quickly as you can, 5 4 3 2 1. Focus on the next point, focus on the next game, focus on the next speech. Don't give yourself the time to think about what went wrong the last time. You are only as good as your present performance, not your past.

I believe that you will achieve wonderful things in life you are able to crush those negative thoughts and enhance your mental strength.

Chapter 19:

Happy People Give Freely

"For it is in giving that we receive." - Saint Francis of Assisi.

A Chinese saying goes by, "If you want happiness for an hour, take a nap. If you want happiness for a day, go fishing. If you want happiness for a year, inherit a fortune. If you want happiness for a lifetime, help somebody." It is indeed better to give than to receive. Scientific research provides compelling anecdotal evidence that giving is a powerful pathway to personal growth and lasting happiness. When we give freely, our brain stimulates endorphins and blesses us with a feeling of euphoria. Altruism is hardwired in our brains and tends to provide us with pleasure. Helping others is a secret to living a happier and healthier, wealthier, productive, and more meaningful life.

Whether it's a charity, a piece of advice, a helping hand of any sort, or supporting someone throughout their journey, researchers Dunn, Aknin, Akin, and Norton performed a study. They showed that there is, in fact, a link between generosity and happier life. The gesture of caring about other people and doing something to improve their quality of life is the source of happiness. Once you start giving, you will feel more content and happier, and there will be no going back. You will get addicted to helping others and to the feeling that follows.

A group of psychologists from the University of California Santa Barbara conducted a study to ascertain if generosity is part of human nature. The observation showed that being a giver is more fulfilling than being a receiver and that generosity is deeply embedded in our systems. "You don't need to become a self-sacrificing martyr to feel happier. Just being a little more generous will suffice," says Prof. Tobler.

High-generosity respondents appeared not only happier but happier more often. This overarching sense of happiness in high-generosity individuals may positively affect their higher likelihood of finding life more meaningful. They were also 20% more likely to be optimistic about their future, be proud of themselves, and find enjoyment in their jobs. It's no secret that you have to give a little to get a little. The more generous you are too loved ones, acquaintances, or even strangers, the more likely those selfless deeds will be reciprocated sometime down the line. Neuroeconomics found in a recent study that merely promising to be more generous is enough to trigger a change in our brain that will eventually make us happier.

In a 2006 study, Jorge Moll and colleagues at the National Institutes of Health found that when people give, it could be anything; it activates the warm glow effect, regions of the brain associated with pleasure, social connection, and trust. Whatever you are giving to people, society, or nature, you will find yourself benefiting from a hefty dose of happiness in the process. When you express your gratitude in words or actions, you not only boost your positivity but other people's as well. The more we give, the more we stand to gain purpose, meaning, and happiness – all of the things we look for in life but are so hard to find.

Chapter 20:
Saying Yes To Things

Today we're going to talk about why saying yes can be a great thing for you and why you should do so especially in social invites.

Life you see is a funny thing. As humans, we tend to see things one dimensionally. And we tend to think that we have a long life ahead of us. We tend to take things for granted. We think we will have time to really have fun and relax after we have retired and so we should spend all our efforts and energy into building a career right now, prioritising it above all else. When faced with a choice between work and play, sometimes many of us, including myself choose work over social invites.

There were periods in my life that i routinely chose work over events that it became such a habit to say no. Especially as an entrepreneur, the interaction between colleagues or being in social events is almost reduced to zero. It became very easy and comfortable to live in this bubble where my one and only priority in life is to work work work. 24 hours, 7 days a week. Of course, in reality a lot of time was wasted on social media and Netflix, but u know, at least i could sort of pretend that i was kind of working all day. And I was sort of being productive and sort of working towards my goals rather than "wasting time on social events". That was what I told myself anyway.

But life does not work that way. As I prioritised work over all else, soon all the social invite offers started drying up. My constant "nos" were becoming evident to my social circle and I was being listed as perpetually unavailable or uninterested in vesting time or energy into any friendships or relationships. And as i retreated deeper and deeper into this black hole of "working remotely" i found myself completely isolated from new experiences and meeting new people, or even completely stopped being involved in any of my friend's lives.
I've successfully written myself out of life and I found myself all alone in it.

Instead of investing time into any meaningful relationships, I found that my closest friends were my laptop, tablet, phone, and television. Technology became my primary way of interacting with the world. And I felt connected, yet empty. I was always plugged in to wifi, but i lived my life through a screen instead of my own two eyes. My work and bedroom became a shell of a home that I spent almost all my time, and life just became sort of pointless. And I just felt very alone.

As I started to feel more and more like something was missing, I couldn't quite make out what it was that led me to this feeling. I simply though to myself, hey I'm prioritising work and my career, making money is what the internet tells me I should do, and not having a life is simply part of the price you have to pay... so why am I so incredibly unhappy?

As it turns out, as I hope many of you have already figured out at this point, that life isn't really just about becoming successful financially. While buying a house, getting a car, and all that good stuff is definitely something that we should strive towards, we should not do so at the expense of our friends. That instead of saying no to them, we should start saying yes, at least once in a while. We need to signal to our friends that hey, yes even though I'm very busy, but I will make an effort to carve out time for you, so that you know I still value you in my life and that you are still a priority.

We need to show our friends that while Monday may not work for us, that I have an opening maybe 2 weeks later if you're still down. That we are still available to grow this friendship.

I came to a point in my life where I knew something had to change. As I started examining my life and the decisions I had made along the way with regards to my career, I knew that what I did wrong was saying no WAAAAAY too often. As I tried to recall when was the last time I actually when I went out with someone other than my one and only BFF, I simply could not. Of the years that went by, I had either said that I was too busy, or even on the off chances that I actually agreed to some sort of meetup, I had the habit of bailing last minute on lunch and dinner appointments with friends. And I never realized that i had such a terrible reputation of being a flaker until I started doing some serious accounting of my life. I had become someone that I absolutely detested without even realising it. I have had people bail on me at the very last minute before, and I hated that feeling. And whenever someone did that to me, I generally found it difficult to ask them out again because I felt that they weren't really that interested in meeting me anyway. That they didn't even bother to reschedule the appointment. And little did I know, I was becoming that very same person and doing the very thing that I hate to my friends. It is no wonder that I started dropping friends like flies with my terrible actions.

As I came to this revelation, I started panicking. It was as if a truck had hit me so hard that I felt that I was in a terrible accident. That how did I let myself get banged up to that extent?

I started scrolling through my contact lists, trying to find friends that might still want to hang out with me. I realized that my WhatsApp was basically dry as a desert, and my calendar was just work for the last 3 years straight with no meaningful highlights, no social events worth noting.

It was at this point that I knew I had made a huge mistake and I needed to change course immediately. Salvaging friendships and prioritising social activities went to the top of my list.

I started creating a list of friends that I had remotely any connection to in the last 5 years and I started asking them out one by one. Some of my friends who i had asked out may not know this, but at that point in my life, i felt pretty desperate and alone and I hung on to every meeting as if my life depended on it. Whilst I did manage to make some appointments and met up with some of them. I soon realized that the damage had been done. That my friends had clearly moved on without me... they had formed their own friends at work and elsewhere, and I was not at all that important to have anymore. It was too little too late at that point and there was not much I could do about it. While I made multiple attempts to ask people out, I did not receive the same offers from people. It felt clearly like a one-way street and I felt that those people that I used to call friends, didn't really see me as one. You see growing a friendship takes time, sometimes years of consistent meetups before this person becomes indispensable in your life. Sharing unique experiences that allow your friends to see that you are truly vested in them and that you care about them and want to spend time with them. I simply did not give myself that chance to be integrated into someone's life in that same way, I did not invest that time to growing those friendships and I paid the price for it.

But I had to learn all these the hard way first before I can receive all the good that was about to come in the future.

In the next piece, I will show how i actually turned my life around by putting myself in positions where I will be exposed to more chances of social activity. And when saying yes became critical to growing a new social network for myself.

Chapter 21:
7 Ways To Discover Your Strengths

It is a fact that everybody has at least one skill, one talent, and one gift that is unique to them only. Everyone has their own set of strengths and weaknesses. Helen Keller was blind but her talent of speaking moved the world. Stephen Hawking theorised the genesis by sitting paralyzed in a wheelchair. The barber who does your hair must have a gifted hand for setting YOUR hair at reasonable prices—otherwise you wouldn't be visiting them.

See, the thing is, everyone is a prodigy at one thing or another. It's only waiting to be discovered and harnessed. Keeping that fact in mind…

Here are 7 Ways You can Discover Your Potential Strengths and Change Your Life Forever:

1. Try Doing Things That You Have Never Done

Imagine what would have happened if Elvis Presley never tried singing, if Michael Jordan never tried playing basketball or if Mark Zuckerberg never tried coding. These individuals would have been completely different persons, serving different purposes in life. Even the whole world would've been different today if some specific people didn't try doing some specific things in their lives.

Unfortunately, many of us never get to know what we are truly good at only because we don't choose to do new things. We don't feel the need to try and explore things that we have never done before in our lives. As a result, our gifted talents remain undiscovered and many of us die with it. So while the time is high, do as many different things you can and see what suits you naturally. That is how you can discover your talent and afterwards, it's only a matter of time before you put it to good use and see your life change dramatically.

2. Don't Get Too Comfortable With Your Current State

It is often the case that we cling on to our current state of being and feel absolutely comfortable in doing so. In some cases, people may even embrace the job that they don't like doing only because 'it pays enough'. And honestly, I totally respect their point of view, it's up to people what makes them happy. But if you ask me how one can discover their hidden talents—how one might distinguish oneself—then I'm going to have to say that never get used to doing one particular thing. If one job or activity occupies you so much that you can't even think of something else, then you can never go out to venture about doing new stuff. The key is to get out, or should I say 'break out' from what you are doing right now and move on to the next thing. What is the next thing you might want to try doing before you die? Life is short, you don't want to go on your whole life, never having experienced something out of your comfort bubble.

3. What Is The Easiest Thing You Can Do?

Have you ever found yourself in a place where you did something for the first time and immediately you stood out from the others? If yes, then chances are, that thing might be one of your natural strengths.

If you've seen 'Forrest Gump', you should remember the scene where Forrest plays table-tennis for the first time in a hospital and he's just perfect at the game. "For some reason, ping-pong came very naturally to me, so I started playing it all the time. I played ping-pong even when I didn't have anyone to play ping-pong with.", says Forrest in the movie.

So bottom-line, pay attention to it if something comes about being 'too easy' for you. Who knows, you might be the world's best at it.

4. Take Self-Assessment Tests

There are countless, free self-assessment tests that are available online in all different kinds of formats. Just google it and take as many tests you like. Some of these are just plain and general aptitude tests or IQ tests, personality tests etc. while there are others which are more particular and tell you what type of job is suited for you, what kind of skills you might have, what you might be good at, and those kinds of things. These tests are nothing but a number of carefully scripted questions which reveal a certain result based on how you answered each question. A typical quiz wouldn't take more than 30 minutes while there are some short and long quizzes which might take 15 minutes and 45 minutes respectively.

Though the results are not very accurate, it can do a pretty good job at giving you a comprehensive, shallow idea of who you are and what you can be good at.

5. Make Notes On How You Deal With Your Problems

Everyone faces difficult situations and overcomes them in one way or the other. That's just life. You have problems, you deal with them, you move on and repeat.

But trouble comes in all shapes and sizes and with that, you are forced to explore your problem-solving skills—you change your strategies and tactics—and while at it, sometimes you do things that are extraordinary for you, without even realizing it. John Pemberton was trying out a way to solve his headache problem using Coca leaves and Kola nuts, but incidentally he made the world's coke-drink without even knowing about it. Lesson to be learned, see how YOU deal with certain problems and why is it different from the others who are trying to solve the same problem as you.

6. Ask Your Closest Friends and Family

People who spend a lot of time with you, whether it be your friend, family or even a colleague gets to see you closely, how you work, how you behave, how you function overall. They know what kind of a person you are and at one point, they can see through you in a manner that you yourself never can. So, go ahead and talk to them, ask them what THEY think your strongest suit can be—listen to them, try doing what they think you might turn out to be really good at, Who knows?

7. Challenge Yourself

The growth of a human being directly corresponds to the amount of challenge a person faces from time to time. The more a person struggles, the more he or she grows—unlocks newer sets of skills and strengths. This is a lifelong process and there's no limit on how far you can go, how high your talents can accomplish.

Now, one might say, "what if I don't have to struggle too much? What if my life is going easy on me?". For them, I'd say "invite trouble". Because if you are eager to know about your skills and strengths (I assume you are since you're reading this), you must make yourself face difficulties and grow from those experiences. Each challenge you encounter and overcome redefines your total strength.

Final Thoughts

To sum it up, your life is in your hands, under your control. But life is short and you gotta move fast. Stop pursuing what you are not supposed to do and set out to find your natural talents RIGHT NOW. Once you get to know your strengths, you will have met your purpose in life.

Chapter 22:
Happy People are Okay with Not Being Okay

All of us have a tendency where we constantly try to make people feel better about ourselves. We are fundamentally driven by empathy and compassion but what happens often is that these two are misdirected. Then we put our idea of okay onto other people and ourselves. Have you ever wondered what would it feel like when we simply whatever comes our way? When we are physically sick, of course, we take medicines to feel better, but there are also times when we are in emotional pain, and then we have no medicine to take and what happens is we seek out a solution, and that puts off the process where we can feel our feelings.

If you go through a breakup and do not allow yourself to feel the pain, what you will do is harm the next person you will date or sabotage your relationship with them. What will heal your wound is actively processing your emotions. This is not at all going to be comfortable, but it is essential for your emotional growth. What you need to do is start shedding the shame that surrounds not being okay. Just because you are in pain and not at the top of your work does not mean that you are weak. You also need to know that you are not the only one who thinks like that. We have been conditioned in this way of dysfunctional thinking and feeling. Most of us think that this is normal and normal is fine, but if you talk about health, that is a different story.

Of course, there are actions that you take that help you release the emotional pain you are in, but you have to remember that almost all of these actions will ask you to focus on yourself before you start focusing on others—for example, yoga. Yoga teaches you that your pain is not permanent, and it also tells us about how we have to be in an uncomfortable pose for a while to release that pain.

You have to remember that the only focus over here is you and you alone, but because we are all on a journey, we do get wind up in others' problems, which helps us find profound connections with them. It is okay to feel scared, or to feel pain, to feel uncertain, to feel lonely, to feel grief, it is okay to not be okay, and these are some of the things that you should never forget.

All the pain that you are feeling right now is not permanent. It will eventually pass. What you can do is honour your emotional experience by not avoiding it and being present for it; you should not try to distract yourself with every fibre of your being. This is a process that will help you heal and grow and move forward on this road. Show up for whatever you feel, even if it is just for a day.

Chapter 23:
Live Life To The Fullest

Have you ever felt like others don't understand your pain when they seem to be living a happy life? You're not alone in feeling this way, but the truth is that happiness takes work, and learning how to live life to the fullest takes dedication and practice.

People who smile in public have been through every bit as much as people who cry, frown, and scream. They just simply found the courage and strength to smile through it and enjoy life in the best way possible.

Life is short, and we only live once. Learning to live life to the fullest is an important step in making the most of every day.

Whether it's taking care of your children, working hard on your career, writing a new blog post each day, or baking up fabulous creations, you get to decide how you enjoy spending your time. Your parents, friends, community, and society in general all have their opinions, but at the end of the day, you're the only person who will be around for every moment of your life.

Do what makes you happy, and everything else will fall into place. This may not mean finding your perfect job if you're limited by education, location, or job openings. However, you can still do what you love by engaging in hobbies, volunteer work, or mentoring.

Sometimes there's danger involved in life, but every reward carries risk with it. If you never take risks, you'll never get anywhere in life, and you certainly won't learn how to live life to the fullest.

Staying in your comfort zone is the fastest way to become discontent Without stepping outside what you're already comfortable with, you will cease to learn and stagnate in both your personal and professional life. While it may feel uncomfortable, taking a risk can be as simple as saying yes next time your friends want to go out instead of staying at home alone. It can mean going out on a blind date, buying plane tickets to a new city, or dragging out those paints that have been stuffed away for years.

When people look back on their lives, <u>they regret the chances they didn't take</u> more than the ones they did, so find something new to try today and set goals beyond what you currently believe possible.

You'll hear people say, "I had that idea," every time you see someone create something great. Everyone had the idea for Facebook first. The reason Mark Zuckerberg got rich off of it is because he went out and did it while everyone else was talking about it. Learning to live life to the fullest is a big step in discovering a path that will lead you to your greatest sense of happiness and accomplishment. We all need moments to rest and relish in a sense of contentment, but staying in one place too long will leave you feeling a lack in life. Discover what makes your life feel meaningful and go after it.

Chapter 24:
What To Do When You Feel Like Your Work is not Good Enough

Feeling like your work is not good enough is very common; your nerves can get better of you at any time throughout your professional life. There is nothing wrong with nerves; It tells you that you care about improving and doing well. Unfortunately, too much nervousness can lead to major self-doubt, and that can be crippling. You are probably very good at your work, and when even once you take a dip, you think that things are not like how they seem to you. If this is something you're feeling, then you're not alone, and this thing is known as Imposter Syndrome. This term is used to describe self-doubt and inadequacy. This one thing leaves people fearing that there might be someone who will expose them. The more pressure you apply to yourself, the more dislocation is likely to occur. You create more anxiety, which creates more fear, which creates more self-doubt. You don't have to continue like this. You can counter it.

Beyond Work

If your imposter syndrome affects you at work, you should take some time out and start focusing on other areas of your life. There are chances that there is something in your personal life that is hindering your work life. This could be anything your sleep routine, friends, diet, or even your relationships. There is a host of external factors that can affect your performance. If there are some boxes you aren't ticking, then there is a high chance of you not performing well at work.

You're Better Than You Think

When you're being crippled by self-doubt, the first thing you have to think about is why you were hired in the first place. The interviewers saw something in you that they believed would improve the business.

So, do you think they would recruit someone who can't do the job? No, they saw your talent, they saw something in you, and you will come good.

When you find yourself in this position, take a moment to write down a few things that you believe led to you being in the role you are now. What did those recruiters see? What did your boss recognize in you? You can also look back on a period of time where you were clicking and felt victorious. What was different then versus now? Was there an external issue like diet, exercise, socializing, etc.?

Check Yourself Before You Wreck Yourself

A checklist might be of some use to you. If you have a list to measure yourself against, then it gives you more than just one thing to judge yourself against. We're far too quick to doubt ourselves and criticize harshly.

The most obvious checklist in terms of work is technical or hard skills, but soft skills matter, too. It's also important to remember that while you're technically proficient now, things move quickly, and you'll reach a point where everything changes, and you have to keep up. You might not ever excel at something, but you can accept the change and adapt to the best of your ability.

It matters that you're hard-working, loyal, honest, and trustworthy. There's more to judge yourself on than just your job. Even if you make a mistake, it's temporary, and you can fix it.

Do you take criticism well? Are you teachable? Easy to coach? Soft skills count for something, which you can look to even at your lowest point and recognize you have strengths.

When you're struggling through a day, week, or even a month, take one large step backward and think about what it is you're unhappy with. What's causing your unhappiness, and how can you improve it?

It comes down to how well you know yourself. If you're clear on what your values are and what you want out of life, then you're going to be fine. If the organization you work for can't respect your values and harness your strengths, then you're better off elsewhere. So, it is extremely important to take time out for that self check-in there could be times you talk to yourself in negative light. Checking in with yourself regularly and not feeding yourself negativity could be one-step forward.

Chapter 25:
Meditate to Rewire Your Brain for Happiness

Suppose you've ever read the book Bridge to Terabithia (or seen the movie). In that case, you are familiar with Terabithia – an imaginary world that the main characters, Jesse and Leslie, create as a haven. It is somewhere they can go to be free from the cares and worries of the world.

Meditation has given me a Terabithia. I have created a clearing of calm and tranquility that I can enter into within seconds whenever I feel the need. I have a refuge no matter where I am or what I am doing. The worries of the world no longer threaten me. Except this mental place isn't imaginary, and it isn't populated with trolls and wild creatures – it is as real as the world we live in.

Since starting my meditation habit, my brain has been rewired for happiness, peace, and success. Here are just a few of the benefits:

I rarely become angry.

I find happiness in unexpected places.

I form deeper relationships and build friendships more easily.

However, by far, the largest benefit is that a deep, serene calm and peace is slowly permeating into every area of my life. At first, meditating felt unusual – like I was stepping out of normal life and doing something that most people find strange. I soon realized, however, that this wasn't true – millions of people meditate, and many successful people attribute part of their success to meditation.

Oprah Winfrey, Hugh Jackman, Richard Branson, Paul McCartney, Angelina Jolie... Any of these names sound familiar? All of these are famous meditators.

This list alone is powerful, but maybe you need a little more convincing that meditation is something you should try.

Michael Jordan, Kobe Bryant, Misty-May Trainor, and Derek Jeter are just a few successful athletes who rely on meditation to get them in the zone.

Rupert Murdoch, Russell Simons, and Arianna Huffington all practice meditation.

Arnold Schwarzenegger and Eva Mendez are just a couple more celebrities that make meditation a daily habit.

Meditation Reduces Stress

Are you feeling the weight of the world on your shoulders? Meditation is incredibly effective at reducing stress and anxiety. One study found that mindfulness and zen-type meditations significantly reduce stress when practiced over a period of three months. Another study revealed that meditation reduces the density of brain tissue associated with anxiety and worrying. If you want your stress levels to plummet, meditation may be the answer.

Chapter 26:
Overcoming Your Fears

Today we're going to talk about the topic of fears. What fear is and how we can overcome it. Now before we dive into it, let us just take a brief moment to think of or right down what our greatest fears are right now.

Whether it be taking the next step in your relationship, fear of the unknown, fear of quitting your job and not finding another one, fear or death, fear of illnesses, whatever fear that jumps out at you and is just eating at you at the back of your mind, i want you to remember that fear as we go through this video.

So what is fear exactly? Whilst there are many definitions of fear out there, I'm going to take, as usual, my spin on things. And to me fear is simply a negative feeling that you assign to usually a task that you really don't want to do. And most of the time, the fear is of the unknown, that you can't visualise what is going to happen next. You don't know whether the outcome will be good or bad, and you don't know whether it is the right move to make. So this trio of thoughts keep circling round and round and eventually you just decide that you are not going to take any action on it and you just shove it to one side hoping that it goes away. And whilst you may do that temporarily, sometimes even for months, one day you are going to have to come face to face with it again. And when that day comes, you will either be paralysed again or you may again put it off to a later date.

We procrastinate on our fears because we want a sure thing. We want to know what will happen next, and we fear what we don't know.

Now for the fears that we are talking about today, it is something that will affect your life if u don't take action. If it is like a fear of bungee jumping or sky driving, sure that fear is physical and very real, but also you can make a choice not to do it and your problem is solved. It will not affect your life in a negative way if u don't do it.

But if it is a fear of a career switch because you already hate your job so much and are totally miserable, that is a fear that you should do your best to try and address as soon as possible.

So what can and should you do about these sorts of fears? The answer for this one is not going to be that difficult. Simply think of the consequences of not conquering your task and how much it might prevent you from moving forward in life and you have got your answer.

When the pain associated with not accomplishing the task becomes greater than the fear we assign to it, it is the tipping point that we need to finally take that action. But instead of waiting to get to that excruciating pain, we can visualise and project what it could potentially feel like if we don't do it now and the pain we might feel at a later day, say 1 year from now, when we have wasted another full year of our life not taking that leap of faith, the time we have burned, the time we can never get back, and the opportunity cost of not taking action now, we might just decide that we don;t want to wait until that day comes and face that huge amount of regret that we should've done something a lot sooner.

And what we need to simply do is to just take action. Taking action is something you will hear from all the gurus you will find out there. When faced with a fear or challenge, instead of wondering what dangers lurk in the unknown, just take action and let the experience tell you whether it was indeed the right or wrong decision. Do you necessary homework and due diligence beforehand and take that calculated step forward instead of procrastinating on it. Life is too short to be mucking around. Just go for it and never live your life in fear or regret ever again.

I challenge each and everyone of you to go through the list that we have created at the start of the video. The one that you have been most fearful of doing. And i want you to assess the pros and cons of each fear that you have written down. If there are more pros than cons, i want you to set a deadline for yourself that you will take action on it. And that deadline is today. Don't waste precious time worrying and instead spend more time doing.

Chapter 27:
How To Deal With Impatience.

"The big challenge with impatience is that it's largely justifiable. The way you respond, however, may not be." - Matt Christensen.

Why is he talking so loudly? Why is she walking so slowly? Why isn't he doing his chores? We have all been hit with the impatient nerve now and then. Although these situations aren't avoidable, how we deal and communicate with them counts in the end. The impatience that vibrates through our body can easily make us angry or result in other unpleasant reactions. It can get triggered by a phrase, behavior, or task that often stems from strength, anxiety, or related outside factors. Becoming more patient takes more time.

Dealing with impatience is surely hectic, but it's not that difficult once you master some techniques. The first thing to do when you're being impatient is to take several deep breaths. Our brains tend to go into a fight or flight situation whenever they sniff danger. As a result, hyperventilation or shortage of oxygen occurs. You start getting more excited and stressed and take quick, short breaths that do more harm than good. The best solution is to give yourself time and take a few seconds to breathe deeply. Catch your impatience with a productive response by calming and controlling your mind and body.

The next thing after relaxing your mind is to relax your muscles. When you feel impatient, give attention to your muscles by doing progressive muscle relaxation. Sit comfortably in a position and meditate. Stretch your arms and legs, and then stretch all of your tensed points one by one. Try to relax as much as you can. You will end up feeling calm, and the feeling of impatience will vanish.

We have all heard how communication is the key to dealing with almost everything. It can be fulfilling and productive to speak up about what's making you impatient and what's bothering you. But beware! It would help if you practiced tact and finesse to make sure you don't sound like a jerk when talking about your impatience-ness. Voicing your views out loud is an essential step in combating impatience. Acknowledging your feelings would also open doors for you to ask for help.

Impatience also thrives on disconnection. If not given the appropriate validation, it can be a recipe for a meltdown. Validation, both verbal and non-verbal responses, can communicate understanding, which can further facilitate connection. Validation can taper your impatience by helping shape your behavior and communication.

Dwelling on the feeling of being impatient can get you nowhere. It doesn't provide you with any sense of productiveness, helpfulness, or pleasantness. Rather than being caught up in the immediate goal, we must keep reminding ourselves to keep a larger perspective of the situation.

Always be mindful of your situations and trust your instinct to deal with your problems. Some people become impatient because of underlying unresolved issues, such as anger, perfectionism, and depression/anxiety. Try helping yourself with acceptance and commitment therapy, anger management, or CBT if you think you are caught up in these feelings. Remember, being patient can get you so many places, while being impatient will have you stuck in one!

Chapter 28:
What Are You Measuring In Your Life?

Do you know your long game? Do you know what is that single thing that you want to keep for a long time? Do you have the simple and straight process to keep your life on track? What is it that you are searching for in your life?

You see, we all are living our lives in certain ways. We all are having a routine that suites us individually. But we don't know if we are actually making a change in our life or not!

Take this for an example. You are hired by a company as a senior manager. You work in that company for a year or so. You are following all the basic duties required of you. You have notable respect that comes with your position. But on what metrics can you say that this respect is what people give you for your dedicated word and not because you are someone's boss.

We might be earning a lot of money, but we cannot say for sure that we have everything we want in life. We might be making wealth upon wealth but we cannot ensure happiness and satisfaction in our life.

So what are we earning in our life for real? What is it that we want to do that will make us look back and smile for everything that happened to us because of some smart decisions?

So start counting today! Take notes for everything even remotely quantifiable!

Numbers aren't just random figures, but they can be a source of satisfaction when we see a rise in certain cases.

You want to look out for newer ways to keep and grow the excitement in life where you don't have to work continuously and deliberately for good results, but your regular activities keep the cycles going.

Take this for an example. If you are relying on people to make you happy, or if you are falsifying the true numbers and manipulating the opinions. You are at great risk of being stripped off of all the real respect you might have ever had.

You can be the New York Times Best Seller. You can be the Best Seller on Amazon but, it will matter to you in the long game of life if you did all that with raw effort and raw ratings of your average reader.

You cannot have a happy life unless you have had a life full of adversity. You cannot be truly sure of everything unless you have gone through everything.

There are a lot of other things in life too, that are much more important than any other aspect of our lives. Things like Love, Morality, Purpose of life, and meaning for everything that we end up doing.

These things need to be measured but the harder we try, the more we end up hurting someone else who is emotionally attached to us.

So keep a check of your environment for the things that matter to you the most, because you and only you will be the best judge of that trait and that other person in your life.

Chapter 29: Develop Mental Toughness In The Face of Adversity

The drawback of this technological revolution that we live in is that we have created a weaker generation, a weaker society. We need everything to be perfect, to be exactly the way we want it to be.

We can't bear a single change in our routines. We can't handle a single harmless task that might test us in any way possible. We can't forgive anyone's mistake but we want all our blunders to be erased.

We can't handle the fact that life is always a step ahead of us. And if something bad happens, we try to mask it. We never try to actually deal with the problems, rather keep them at bay as long as we can.

We are so afraid of trying the do the things that would matter, but we become the wisest when we mock or advise someone else.

We are never truly prepared for the hard times. We are always in a constant fight with our own minds, neglecting reality and creating a false scenario where everything is alright. It is not Alright!

We are living in a time where everyone is in search of greatness. There are more and more people coming into this world every day and the competition is getting harder than it ever was. The day will come when we would have to fight for even the basic necessities of life.

The day might come when we will fail at almost everything we are doing right now. What will we do then?

Life gives us second chances, but those chances require us to be stronger. Those chances want us to first create some chances beforehand before we go forward with the grand scheme.

Chances present themselves to the people who are in the constant struggle to live every minute as if it were their last.

If someone was to ask you to join them for a morning run, you might be enthusiastic for one day. You will wake up at five in the morning, gear up, and go for 10 miles for the first day. On the second day, you will go for it again. A week later you will take a break for a day. A month later you might get a treadmill because you feel more comfortable running in your home rather than going out in the cold mornings. But eventually, you will stop doing it.

All of this is because you are not ready to get out of your comfort zone or not ready to commit for long enough to achieve what you started for.

Learn to say 'No' to 'No'. The day you start saying no to everything that will keep you in your warm cozy bed, is the day you will finally realize what you will achieve that day.

Life will always be hard on you, but you can join the league of successful beings if you stay true to your cause and keep pushing and digging till you finally find the gem of your choice.

Chapter 30:
How to Face Difficulties in Life

Have you noticed that difficulties in life come in gangs attacking you when you're least prepared for them? The effect is like being forced to endure an unrelenting nuclear attack.

Overcoming obstacles in life is hard. But life is full of personal challenges, and we have to summon the courage to face them. These test our emotional mettle — injury, illness, unemployment, grief, divorce, death, or even a new venture with an unknown future. Here are some strategies to help carry you through:

1. Turn Toward Reality

So often, we turn away from life rather than toward it. We are masters of avoidance! But if we want to be present—to enjoy life and be more effective in it—we must orient ourselves toward facing reality. When guided by the reality principle, we develop a deeper capacity to deal with life more effectively. What once was difficult is now easier. What once frightened us now feels familiar. Life becomes more manageable. And there's something even deeper that we gain: Because we can see that we have grown stronger, we have greater confidence that we can grow even stronger still. This is the basis of feeling capable, which is the wellspring of a satisfying life.

2. Embrace Your Life as It Is Rather Than as You Wish It to Be

The Buddha taught that the secret to life is to want what you have and do not want what you don't have. Being present means being present to the life that you have right here, right now. There is freedom in taking life as it comes to us—the good with the bad, the wonderful with the tragic, the love with the loss, and the life with the death. When we embrace it all, then we have a real chance to enjoy life, value our experiences, and mine the treasures that are there for the taking. When we surrender to the reality of who we are, we give ourselves a chance to do what we can do.

3. Take Your Time

As the story of the tortoise and the hare tells us, slow and steady wins the race. By being in a hurry, we actually thwart our own success. We get ahead of ourselves. We make more mistakes. We cut corners and pay for them later. We may learn the easy way but not necessarily the best way. As an old adage puts it: The slower you go, the sooner you get there. Slow, disciplined, incremental growth is the kind of approach that leads to lasting change.

Chapter 31:
How Not To Control Everything

Steve Maraboli once said, "You must learn to let go. Release the stress. You were never in control anyway." Now, it goes without saying that things flow much more smoothly when you give up control when you let them be natural when you allow them to happen instead of making them happen. Being a control freak can drain so much of your mental energy without you even knowing it. It can cause you to fall into a never-ending loop of overthinking. We obsess over controlling every aspect of life without realizing the negative effects it can cause to our health, goals, and relationships. We grab them so tightly until we suffocate and kill them eventually.

Mastering the art of letting go and not controlling everything is not easy, but we should trust our instincts and know that it will be okay no matter the circumstances. We should always open ourselves to opportunities and possibilities. The path that we control and attach ourselves desperately to isn't always the right one. There would be other valuable and productive paths if we naturally and smoothly sail onto them. Letting go of control means more freedom, peace, joy, support, and connection. It will be hard at first, but once you get your hands on it, it'll become easier and easier for you.

The first and foremost thing to do is to use your imagination. We often find ourselves overthinking the worst possibilities that could happen to us. It's like using all of your energy, time and head on climbing the steepest mountain when you can take the stairs easily and free yourself from all the stress. So, the next time you find yourself in a controlling mindset, think of all the emotional and physical energy that you might drain in trying to control a simple situation. Embrace the freedom of not having to climb that mountain and just let go and wait for whatever it is that's going to happen.

Control is usually rooted in fear. But, understand that fear is merely an illusion, its false evidence may appear real, but it's very much fake. We control things because we fear what might happen if we don't. We attach ourselves to expectations and then set ourselves up for disappointment. So, focus on grounding yourself. Take a walk in the park, meditate, relax your mind. The positive energy will only flow in when the negative energy flows out.

Have a firm belief in yourself and practice saying affirmations. Deduct any self doubts that you have and keep reassuring yourself. Recognize the importance of freedom and see what it means to you. Once you start enjoying your space, the act of controlling everything will begin to annoy you.

Change your views about life. Could you work with your life, not against it? The sooner you realize that life is beautiful and on your side, the easier it will be for you not to control everything. You would be open to opportunities and would accept whatever it will give you. If life is moving you in one direction, instead of wasting your energy in resisting and fighting it, embrace it and work towards its betterment. Some things are beyond our control; only control what you can and let go of what you cannot.

Chapter 32:
10 Habits Of Happy Kids

Happy kids are unique from their peers. They are joyous throughout and it spreads even to those around them. You cannot help but love them for their charming young personality. Here are ten habits of happy kids:

1. They Love Immensely

Happy kids do not withhold their love for people who thrill them. They love deeply and it is difficult to turn them against the people they love. They always want to be carried by them and play together at the slightest opportunity.

The love of happy kids is genuine. They show their love through small acts like wanting to follow them everywhere and clinging to them when they want to leave.

2. They Easily Make Friends

Happy kids have no problem forging friendships with both their peers and adults. Their happiness attracts people to them and they get along quickly. They have a magnetic influence wherever they go.

Their loving nature coupled with a joyous attitude makes socializing with other people an easy task. Happy kids are popular in their circles for their warm friendship.

3. They Have No Sense Of Insecurity

Happy kids are not insecure. They have a sense of belonging to the family they are raised in and in the groups they belong to. They are not afraid that somebody else can replace them or that others will be favorites and overtake them.

They are self-confident and are not threatened by any competition from anybody. At their young age, it is noticeable that they promote the welfare of other children too.

4. They Are Fast Learners

Most happy kids are by default fast learners too. Although there are a few who are happy but slow learners, a majority of them quickly grasp concepts that skip the attention of unhappy kids.

Their fast learning is attributed to their positive attitude. They are eager to make things work for them and they learn fast using the most convenient method. Unlike happy kids, the unhappy ones have no interest in a majority of things happening around them making them learn associated concepts slower.

5. They Have Enough Sleep

Happy kids are not deprived of sleep. Their sleeping schedule is on time as advised by pediatricians and experienced parents. They have no insomnia that is often caused by restlessness, emotional and mental stress.

Unlike adults, kids are supposed to have a night of uninterrupted peaceful sleep for many hours. Unhappy kids have underlying factors that cause insomnia. It is a red flag that parents and guardians should address.

6. They Are Positive

Happy kids have a positive attitude towards life. They are free from stress and worry. When you pay attention to conversation among kids of the same age group, you can single out those who are happy in the manner they talk. Everything is possible to them.

Happy kids have a positive view of life and they believe that the adults in their lives can easily solve their problems. Their positivity is admirable.

7. They Are Very Creative

Happy kids are very creative. Their minds are not clogged by a lot of things and they have room to think of innovations at their age unlike their unhappy peers and adults too who are constantly worried about the source of their next provisions.

Creativity breeds in their positive attitude. They want to make life better at their level. Their innovations are simple yet a good sign of a promising kid.

8. They Explore Their Talents At A Very Young Age

Happy kids discover their passion at an early age because their happiness leads them to engage in activities they love. Parents and guardians guide them in exploring their talents and support them by buying toys for the things their children love.

Their happiness makes them enthusiastic to try new things and they eventually discover their talents. Under the right tutelage, they make very good professionals in the sectors they settle in.

9. They Eat Well

What is the connection between feeding habits and the happiness of a child? Happy kids have peace of mind that subconsciously improves their appetite.

Most stressed kids have a poor appetite because their minds are occupied with how to address the challenges they are undergoing. They eat because it's meals time and they do not want to be isolated but not because they are hungry.

10. They Have Good Health Practices

Happy kids are healthy. They are stress-free and eat well. They hardly fall sick because their immunity is not compromised. Their parents guide them in eating healthy foods and observing hygiene. This keeps diseases at bay.

Having good health contributes to their happiness because they are not in pain caused by sickness.

In conclusion, these minute habits of happy kids are mostly ignored but play a big role in their growth. Initiate them in your child and watch the transformation.

Chapter 33:
Five Habits That Can Make Someone Like You

Favor and love are won. It is an endless race in life that requires zeal. You have to appeal to the other person so that they can like you back and return some affection. We often struggle to make those around us realize that we like them. Sometimes we succeed and at other times, we learn (not lose). The struggle is real and we need to measure up to the task.

Here are five habits that can make someone like you:

1. Compliment Them Genuinely

Do not underestimate the power of a simple compliment on someone. A compliment is an indication that you recognize the other person's excellence in something. Appreciate their dressing, skills, effort or assistance lent to you by saying a 'thank you or you look amazing today!' When you make people feel loved by often genuinely complimenting them, they get motivated and feel loved. Always give genuine compliments and avoid faking them because it may come out as envy or jealousy. Instead of building bridges with the other person, you would have unknowingly built a wall.

Wouldn't you like someone who genuinely compliments you? Of course, you would. The glory that fills your heart when you are complimented will draw you to the other person. Genuine compliments are given in private or public. It is hypocritical to wait to be in public before you compliment someone. There is no occasion for acknowledging another. As long as it is in their presence, do not shy away from it.

2. Support Their Initiatives

Be in the front line to support the businesses and initiatives of those you want to court their attention. Be in their cheering squad and support their businesses and careers in whatever capacity. To be able to make someone like you, first court their attention, and what better way is there than to show up in those activities that matter to them?

If you develop the habit of being their ambassador in their businesses, they will see that you both have aligned goals and may take a keen interest in you. Their liking for you will grow as you appreciate their work and interests. Supporting their initiatives also means advising them on matters you are competent in. Your input should not be sycophancy but aimed at making a change.

Those you want to like you will do so in appreciation of your invaluable input in their work. Your ties will be stronger and they will like you more beyond your unconditional support. Be careful to maintain the relationship between you two. It is fragile more so that you are the one initiating it and it is up to them to fall for it.

3. Stand Up For Them

What can your friends say about you in your absence? This is a rare quality that most people look for when searching for potential friends or associates. If you want someone to like you, stand up for them in their absence. Your testimony about them to other people should be positive, one that will inspire their love for you.

You cannot possibly expect someone to like you if you speak negatively about them behind their back. Your words will haunt you should the one you intended for hears it. It should be something that you can confidently repeat to their face. Your sanctity will make you stand out when you stand up for your friends (pun intended).

Standing up for people you want to like you is a good way of 'shouting' your support for them. They will rush to see who it is that defended their character in public and will develop a special liking for you. Furthermore, you should do this in a manner that attracts respect and decorum to the one you are publicly defending.

4. Be Dignified

You are what you attract. It begins with your attributes and how you carry yourself around. This plays a significant role in the perception of other people towards you. What is their opinion about you? Is it desirable enough to make them like you? Work on how you present yourself to other people and you will be irresistibly likable.

There is never a second chance to make a first impression. It is up to you to ensure that the first impression which sticks is the correct one. Carry yourself with dignity in everything you do because you never know who is watching. Random strangers will automatically like you as they observe your personal and public life.

5. Be Humble

Humility is a rare virtue in most people. Nobody wants to be associated with violent friends because their rage makes them unpredictable. Humbleness does not mean you have allowed people to mistreat you. It means you are intelligent enough to choose your battles wisely.

Humble people are likable to a fault. People are attracted to calm personalities. They look mature, responsible, and chaos-free. Portray a positive image of yourself and you will be amazed at how people will like you.

Incorporating these five habits in your routine will make people like you and the icing of the cake is that whoever you aim to like you could be among them.

Chapter 34:
10 Habits Of Happy People

Happiness is a state of joy. In happiness, one is thrilled, contented, and tickled by joy. It is often expressed through bursts of laughter amidst smiles and it cannot be hidden. Happiness is a state everyone desires but few can maintain. Here are ten habits of happy people:

1. **They Are Outgoing**

Happy people are very social. They easily interact with strangers and make friends faster than ordinary people. They are charming to a fault and you cannot help but love their company.

Happy people are easily noticeable in a room full of different people. They are conspicuously outgoing to initiate trips, vacations, and team-building activities. Their social nature makes them thrive both in outdoor and indoor interactions.

2. **They Are Self-Driven**

Happy people have a strong personality that drives them in life. They are not coerced to do something and often act out of self-will. They stand out from a population that requires much convincing before they act.

They live a purposeful life that is crystal in their minds. Happy people do not need an external influence to be happy. They genuinely derive pleasure from what they do.

3. They Wake Up Early

Happy people know the secret of waking up early and do not need persuasion to wake up earlier than everybody else.

In waking up early, they keep off conflict with other people who could ruin their day. They build the foundation of the day ahead of them in the morning and they can maintain the tempo until the end. Strangers can do very little to ruin their happiness.

4. They Are Positive About Life

Happy people are very optimistic about life. Positivity is their middle name. They hardly entertain thoughts of failure. Like all of us, happiness is a choice they have to constantly make and work towards it. It distinguishes them from everyone else.

How can you be happy if you do not see the good out of the ugly? Happy people look at the brighter side of life because the grass is not greener on the other side but where you water it.

5. They Keep The Company Of Other Happy People

Happy people keep the fire of happiness burning because they associate with like-minded people. They share ideas and strategies on how to pursue their purpose. They also encourage each other when hope is bleak.

The company of sad and angry people is devastating because it gives no room for happiness to thrive. Happy people embrace each other's company because it is all they have got if they are to stay happy.

6. They Read Success Stories

Success stories are inspiring. They make us pull our socks and give us hope to succeed as others have. Happy people read and share success stories because therein lies happiness. They bask in the glory of their friends because they believe their turn too shall come.

Happy people shun bad news and stories of despair because they are discouraging and one could succumb to depression if they are not careful.

7. They Know How To Handle Bad News And Rejection

Happy people know that rejection does not spell doom for them. They have hope that they can rise above all challenges they face and still be happy. Unlike ordinary people who take rejection personally and despair, happy people consider it as another phase of life.

Handling bad news is a skill that happy people have perfected. Although some bad news could hit them hard, they know how to soak in their happiness and not live in sadness.

8. They Are Agents Of Change

Happy people are agents of change wherever they go. They make a difference with their speech and their aura changes everything. Everybody can feel the impact of happy people wherever they are.

Happy people inspire others to be like them. They recruit others in their league of happiness because they desire to see a changing world.

9. They Are Loving And Caring

Happy people can afford to be caring because they have no traces of bitterness or anger within them. They genuinely care for the welfare of other people.

Happiness makes people loving unlike those who harbor anger. You can only give what you have and it is natural for happy people to care more and sad people hurt more.

10. They Live An Authentic Lifestyle

Authenticity is a mark of happy people. They live a genuine lifestyle without seeking to impress anyone. Their joy does not lie in the approval of strangers but the satisfaction of their needs.

Happy people live within their financial means and not in the standards that other people have put for them. Their priorities are independent of external influence.

In conclusion, happy people are easy to spot. It is everybody's dream to be happy but a very elusive one. These ten habits of happy people distinguish them from others.

Chapter 35:
3 Steps To Choose Mind Over Mood

Have you ever said something out of anger that you later regretted? Do you let fear talk you out of taking the risks that could really benefit you? If so, you're not alone.

Emotions are powerful. Your mood determines how you interact with people, how much money you spend, how you deal with challenges, and how you spend your time.

Gaining control over your emotions will help you become mentally stronger. Fortunately, anyone can become better at choosing their mind over their mood. Just like any other skill, managing your emotions requires practice and dedication. Managing your emotions isn't the same as suppressing them. Ignoring your sadness or pretending you don't feel pain won't make those emotions go away.

In fact, unaddressed emotional wounds are likely to get worse over time. And there's a good chance suppressing your feelings will cause you to turn to unhealthy coping skills--like food or alcohol. It's important to acknowledge your feelings while also recognizing that your emotions don't have to control you. If you wake up on the wrong side of the bed, you can take control of your mood and turn your day around. If you are angry, you can choose to calm yourself down.

Here are three ways to gain better control over your mood:

1. Label Your Emotions

Before you can change how you feel, you need to acknowledge what you're experiencing right now. Are you nervous? Do you feel disappointed? Are you sad?

Keep in mind that anger sometimes masks emotions that feel vulnerable--like shame or embarrassment. So pay close attention to what's really going on inside of you.

Put a name your emotions. Keep in mind you might feel a whole bunch of emotions at once--like anxious, frustrated, and impatient.

Labeling how you feel can take a lot of the sting out of the emotion. It can also help you take careful note of how those feelings are likely to affect your decisions.

2. Reframe Your Thoughts

Your emotions affect the way you perceive events. If you're feeling anxious and you get an email from the boss that says she wants to see you right away, you might assume you're going to get fired. If however, you're feeling happy when you get that same email, your first thought might be that you're going to be promoted or congratulated on a job well done.

Consider the emotional filter you're looking at the world through. Then, reframe your thoughts to develop a more realistic view.

If you catch yourself thinking, "This networking event is going to be a complete waste of time. No one is going to talk to me and I'm going to look like an idiot," remind yourself, "It's up to me to get something out of the event. I'll introduce myself to new people and show interest in learning about them."

Sometimes, the easiest way to gain a different perspective is to take a step back and ask yourself, "What would I say to a friend who had this problem?" Answering that question will take some of the emotion out of the equation so you can think more rationally.

If you find yourself dwelling on negative things, you may need to change the channel in your brain. A quick physical activity, like going for a walk or cleaning off your desk, can help you stop ruminating.

3. Engage in a Mood Booster

When you're in a bad mood, you're likely to engage in activities that keep you in that state of mind. Isolating yourself, mindlessly scrolling through your phone, or complaining to people around you are just a few of the typical "go-to bad mood behaviors" you might indulge in.

But, those things will keep you stuck. You have to take positive action if you want to feel better.

Think of the things you do when you feel happy. Do those things when you're in a bad mood and you'll start to feel better.

Here are a few examples of mood boosters:

- Call a friend to talk about something pleasant (not to continue complaining).
- Go for a walk.
- Meditate for a few minutes.
- Listen to uplifting music.

Keep Practicing Your Emotional Regulation Skills

Managing your emotions is tough at times. And there will likely be a specific emotion--like anger--that sometimes gets the best of you.

But the more time and attention you spend on regulating your emotions, the [mentally stronger](#) you'll become. You'll gain confidence in your ability to handle discomfort while also knowing that you can make healthy choices that shift your mood.

Chapter 36:
Stop Thinking and Start Doing

What is going on around you right now? I am not asking this rather telling you because I know most of you are already thinking the same question. You should be asking this question, or should you?

We are a two-faced species. We say something upfront but we adopt the opposite for ourselves at the same time. We want to install a certain methodology in everyone around us but we are ashamed to do the same thing ourselves.

Fear is a more appropriate and less offending word some might say. But why is it? Is something harmful, or something that doesn't make sense only when you yourself are in the same place as others that followed you?

So show off when we don't have something good to contribute in our own lives? Why be a hypocrite who doesn't even have the guts to admit that they are the timidest and lucid person and they want to follow their own instincts?

You have to make those small changes in your life. That will one day result in a bigger change and elevate your life to that ultimate stature, then you are probably dead.

Stop preaching, stop playing around, stop thinking, worrying, wondering, doubting fearing, hoping for some easy way out! Learn to say STOP to everything that goes against your instincts and your wishes for a better tomorrow.

Do you think you are grinding away yourself every day so you deserve a break? No!

What makes you think you have achieved all you can?

Sure you have done a lot in your life, sometimes it was due to circumstances, sometimes your talents, and sometimes just pure luck. But you went through it then and you were very less competent back then! So why can't you do some more things like those, just easier?

You can and you will! Because now you have grown within and have more experience to tackle what needs to be tackled.

If you keep telling yourself and keep thinking, "Oh this wasn't meant to happen", or "Was it my fault?", or "Why does it always have to be me?", you will quite look over your shoulder searching for the easy way out!

Learn to live by the chances that you keep getting every day. Because is too short to be wondering and never to lift a finger and point in the direction of what needs to be done.

Don't act like you are totally blank and have no idea what to do next. Take a moment and your instincts will naturally take you to the best possible solution.

But you have to get up, go out and start pursuing. Because you are your first priority, always was and always should be.

There is a time in everyone's life when they just need to stop thinking and start doing. That time is always the previous second. The day you understand this puzzle, give yourself a tap on the shoulder because you have finally outgrown yourself

www.ingramcontent.com/pod-product-compliance
Lightning Source LLC
Chambersburg PA
CBHW050505120526
44589CB00047B/2363